Explaining Salvation to CHILDREN

Explaining Salvation to CHILDREN

HELPING A CHILD TO RECEIVE CHRIST AS SAVIOR

by

MARJORIE SODERHOLM, M.A.

PREFACE

CHILDREN have talked about accepting Christ over and over again.

Young people have mentioned going to an altar repeatedly as children, but having accepted Christ as Savior several years after these childhood experiences.

Adults have said, "More than one evangelist counted me as a convert when I was a child."

Christian leaders have expressed a need for printed materials to help in explaining salvation to children.

Because of these, I write.

In a pamphlet of so few pages, much must be left unsaid. May what is said be of help to all those who are spending themselves in guiding children in their knowledge of Jesus Christ.

—Marjorie Soderholm

CONTENTS

I. WHY CHILDREN ARE CONFUSED

"I'VE BEEN saved seven times."

"I got saved at camp again this year. Every year at camp I get saved."

"I accepted Jesus yesterday, but I want to do it again today."

"I had a fight with my brother. He cried. Now I want to let Jesus in my heart again."

And on and on and on—these are the testimonies of children. These words come from children who have been in Sunday school, in children's Bible story hours, and in other meetings for children. Why do children say such things? What can be done about it? How can salvation be explained to a child so that he is not merely confused? Any teacher who really loves children and wants to see them become Christians cannot help but ask these questions when he hears such remarks from the lips of children. The teacher will be concerned that perhaps the children are not really understanding what is so important to understand—that Christ died for their sin, and that by accepting Him as Savior they belong to Him. He will wonder if perhaps the children with whom he has worked have merely gone through motions and have not really accepted Jesus as their Savior after all.

*   *   *

WHY DOES a child talk about being saved more than once? There are many reasons. Some are these:

1. He does not understand the terminology that he hears. First he is told that he must be saved; then that he must let Jesus into his heart; next he must give his heart to Jesus;

then he must trust Jesus. Each time he hears a new expression, he thinks he must respond. Thus he "goes forward" every time an invitation is expressed differently from what he last heard.

One adult Christian woman relates how she responded to every invitation given to a group of children when she was a child. She says, "There must be at least a dozen evangelists who count me as one of their converts, but it was not until years later that I actually knew what it meant to be a Christian."

One four-year-old girl was watching a medical program on television with her parents. During the heart operation which was shown she saw the doctors carefully lift out the patient's heart. At that moment she asked, "Daddy, is he giving his heart to Jesus?"

2. He is frightened into a decision. One child said, "I went up there to talk with that man because the teacher said if I didn't I'd go to hell, and I don't want to go there and burn up." Of course a child should know that there is a hell, but he needs to understand that Jesus died not only to save him from hell, but also to keep him from sin now. He needs to realize that it is from the power, not only the penalty, of sin that he is freed. To use hell as the only motivation for accepting Christ as Savior is not being fair to the child, the Scriptures, or the Lord Himself. When a child makes a decision on the basis of fear alone, the scare may soon wear off, and soon he wonders if the whole experience was just something exciting for the moment.

3. He does not understand what sin is; therefore he really sees no need for a Savior. One group of children was having a Bible drill. The teacher asked them to look up Ro-

mans 3:23. They did, and then she asked the question, "How many people have sinned?" They replied, "Everyone." She said, "And that means us, too, doesn't it?" The whole class of third grade boys and girls rose to their feet and cried out surprisedly, "Us?" The teacher realized at that point that children can give the right answer without understanding how it applies to them personally, and that her next task was to make the children aware of sin in their own lives. Without this, the children could not appreciate why Christ died, or what His death on the cross had to do with them.

4. He does not realize that he needs to make his decision to accept Christ as His Savior only once. Everybody tells him that he needs to accept Jesus; therefore he thinks he'd better do it each time someone says that he must. He needs to realize that once he accepts Jesus as his Savior he is in God's family, and that just as he came into his parents' family once, he comes into God's family once.

5. He may at the time he goes forward, so to speak, feel guilty of one particular "naughty thing" that he has done. He asks forgiveness for this one misdeed, mistaking this experience for salvation. Then when he is naughty again, he thinks he must be saved again.

6. He goes for a reward. Sometimes a gift is promised to all those who come to receive Christ as Savior. The child wants the gift; and he follows through the routine of reading a verse and saying a prayer, wondering what that really has to do with the fact that he is going to receive a present. The author was speaking with a third grade girl one time about becoming a Christian. She was using the child's Bible to point out what Christ has done for us. She asked, "Where did you get your Bible?" The child answered, "I was at a

meeting, and the leader said he would give a New Testament to all of us who went to the front to be Christians, so I went." Yet here was that same girl a year later desiring to know how to become a Christian.

7. He follows the crowd. One child raises his hand when an invitation to accept Christ is given. So another child raises his hand, and another; then another, and another. Some who raise their hands may not even know why they are raising them. Just as a child can raise his hand when a question is asked, and then not know the answer, so he can raise his hand in the case of an invitation to accept Christ, too, and yet not know what he has done.

8. He makes his decision on the basis of a story. There are many so-called salvation stories that may cause the child to respond; yet they have very little of the Bible in them. Or if they do have the Scriptures in them, truth and fiction are so interwoven that the child is confused. Later he finds that the story is just a made-up story, and then the part that was Scripture is to him just a part of the story, too. He then has nothing upon which to base his decision, so he thinks he has to be saved again.

9. He wants to please the teacher. The teacher may have said something like this: "Surely you boys and girls will accept Jesus as your Savior for me. I want to see all of you in heaven with me." The child loved his teacher, so he indicated that he did want to be in heaven with his teacher. He was happy because he made his teacher happy. That happy feeling was identified with being saved, but the next week that happy feeling was gone, and so the idea that he is a Christian or that he will be in heaven may be gone, too.

10. He gets tired sitting. The lessons are sometimes

long. The teacher, after one of these long lessons, may ask those who want to become Christians to stand. The child stands. The teacher counts him as being made a convert when he is just being made comfortable.

11. He responds to emotion-packed stories. When a child hears such a story, he wants to cry. He is ready to respond to any question that the teacher poses, without the conviction of the Holy Spirit. The child cries; he feels better. He calls that feeling "being saved," but later he doesn't feel that way any more, so he concludes that he isn't saved either. In many such cases, the child is right in that conclusion. Though he responded, he responded to pressure, and the experience was not real so far as knowing Jesus as Savior is concerned.

12. He had no one to teach him after he did accept Christ. Many children do actually accept Christ as their Savior, but then are left without further direction and teaching. They don't know how to read the Bible; and those who can read it, don't know what to read. They have questions but no one answers them. No one helps them see how the Christian life differs from other lives. No one teaches them how to pray. Before long they doubt, or even forget their experience.

II. BASICS IN TEACHING CHILDREN TO KNOW JESUS CHRIST

WHEN A person realizes how confused a child can become over the wonderful message of salvation in Jesus Christ, he is almost afraid to work with children. It appears to be a dangerous business. And yet children can understand the significance of Christ's death for them personally. They do not have to be confused. They can accept Christ as Savior at even a young age and continue to grow in Him to become mature Christians. Often it is not the message of salvation itself that is confusing to the child. Rather it is the way the message is presented—couched in vocabulary, symbolism, and experiences that are not within the child's experience or understanding. What should one who works with children do in order to help them understand the message of salvation?

There is no formula—no set of questions to ask, no certain six verses to use, no ritual that the child should follow. Yet there are some basics that the teacher should be aware of in order to effectively reach children for Christ. Here are a few. Others will be considered later.

1. The teacher should have clear in his own mind what the child should know in order to appreciate the significance of Christ's death. This should be kept simple, and yet it should be complete. The following might serve as a guide.

God loves you.

You have sinned.

Christ died to pay for your sin.

You must admit to Him that you are a sinner and
ask Him to forgive you.

Then you are in God's family and you have everlasting life.

2. The teacher should be familiar with Scripture that
will help the child see for himself what the Bible teaches.
One group of verses for the guide could be these:

| John 3:16 | Romans 3:23 |
| Romans 5:6 | John 3:36 |

3. The teacher should repeat these truths of the salvation message over and over to children, sometimes emphasizing one, sometimes another facet of the great truth of God's love. This means that the teacher will need to spend much time with the children, rather than trying to pack everything into one story and pressing for a decision.

4. The teacher should be careful to explain the terms he uses. Too often it is taken for granted that the child understands the terminology that the teacher uses. Indeed the child may use the terminology himself, yet when asked what he means he will not know. One must help the child understand the meaning of such terms as *sin, saved, forgiveness, everlasting life,* and *believe.* Sometimes these explanations can be woven right into the lesson or Bible story. Sometimes questions can be asked to see just what the children do understand.

5. The teacher should depend on the Holy Spirit. If the Holy Spirit convicts, the child can make a lasting decision. If the child's decision is because of some one's convincing rather than because of the conviction of the Holy Spirit it will not be genuine. Indeed this kind of decision—only because of pressure—may be harmful in the child's life, for

he later wonders just what his standing with the Lord is. He may not want to admit his confusion because he knows others think he is a Christian; then he lives in turmoil and dissatisfaction.

6. The teacher should explain the salvation message simply. The message should not be hidden in a mass of symbolism. When one word is used to stand for another, such as a *rope* for *sin,* the real message of the Word of God is hidden. The teacher should use these questions to help in the selection of a story or lesson for children:

Do the words mean what they say?

Is the story free from fanciful ideas?

How much of the story is actually the Word of God?

7. The teacher should use the Bible in sharing the message of salvation with children. It is the Word of God, not a made-up story, that conveys the truth of sin and salvation. There are many so-called salvation stories that include a Scripture verse here and there. Yet these stories are not as effective in teaching children as the Word of God itself is. True, it is possible to get the children to respond to these stories, but it is also true that many children later question the response they made.

Bible stories are more direct and more easily explainable than the imaginary, symbolic, made-up stories that are so often used. For instance, it is much easier to help a child understand Nicodemus' confusion at Jesus' words, "Ye must be born again" (John 3) than to help him grasp how a black kerchief stands for sin.

8. The teacher should let the children ask questions. In one third grade class, the children had heard the story of Noah and the Ark for one lesson; the next lesson was Jonah

and the Big Fish. To begin the next lesson, the teacher commented that God had dealt severely with the people in the last two lessons. Then she asked, "Why did God punish the people?" The children answered, "Because of sin." Then teacher and children discussed such questions as:—

What is sin?
What kind of sins do third graders commit?
What can we do about our sin?
What did God do about it?

The children asked such questions as:—

Why do people sin?
Why doesn't God kill the devil?
How can God forgive our sin?
What should we say when we pray?
How can I be a Christian?

When children are allowed to ask questions, they help the teacher sense what their understanding of the Bible is. Also they often ask the questions that give wide-open opportunity to explain salvation. Then the message is not forced. It grows naturally out of a discussion with the children. After this particular discussion, four of the children came to the teacher afterwards asking her to show them how to become Christians. Each one came individually. One came several hours after the discussion was over. There was no pressure. Teacher and children just talked about what God says about sin and salvation, and the Holy Spirit worked through His own Word. As a result several children accepted Christ as their Savior.

9. The teacher should teach God's holiness as well as man's sinfulness. It is true, of course, that we are all sinful; however, if a child receives only this emphasis, he may go

through life satisfied that God forgave his sin without realizing that God expects him to live day by day according to the teaching of the Bible. The child needs to be taught that God is holy and that He expects obedience. He needs instruction as to what God expects in order that his religion and his life may be harmonious.

III. THE PROPER USE OF STORIES IN EXPLAINING SALVATION TO CHILDREN

PREVIOUS REFERENCE has been made to the use of stories in explaining salvation to children. Because it is of central importance to use the Bible, the subject needs further consideration. Often a story similar to this is used:

> Now, boys and girls, I want you to watch very carefully what I do. See, here is my finger. Now I want you to watch this finger. What I am going to do is very important. See, now, I'll dip my finger in this bottle of ink. My, how black my finger is now! How can I get this ink out? Let us try this water. Oh, dear! The water doesn't work. Let us try rubbing the ink off with this towel. My finger is still black. Perhaps I should try cutting off the ink. Oh! I can't do that without taking a part of my finger, too. Well, let's see. Let's try this ink remover. Oh, see, it's coming off. Look, it's gone! You see, boys and girls, there is only one thing that can take away the ink-stain of sin. That is the blood of Jesus Christ. Only His blood can do it. We can't wash it away; we can't rub it off; we can't cut it out! There is only one way. This is serious, children. If you do not get rid of your ink-stain of sin, you will go to hell. How many of you want to get rid of your ink-stain of sin? Raise your hands. Don't wait another day to wash your sin in Jesus' blood.

How would the foregoing story measure up if tested by the three questions given previously for use in selection of a story? Let us measure it.

1. Do the words mean what they say? Is sin an ink-stain? If it is not, why confuse the child by calling it such? How does one wash his sin in Jesus' blood? What does a child do when he washes something? Can he do this with sin?

These are only two examples from the story to point out that it says one thing but means another. A person who already knows the message of salvation can figure out what the symbolism means, but this is actually in the reverse order of what people who use such stories expect. The story is supposed to make the message clear; yet in such a story it takes an understanding of the message to make the story clear.

2. Is the story free from fanciful ideas? Perhaps the idea of cutting out the stain will seem somewhat ridiculous to some children. They know from the beginning that no one is going to do such a thing.

3. How much of the story is actually the Word of God? The story does say that Jesus is the only one who can take away sin. None of the rest of the story is from the Bible. It is made up. Even the one idea from the Scriptures is expressed in such a way that it is difficult for the child to grasp. Even if a child did raise his hand at the end of such a story, one would have to question his understanding of salvation. The reason for questioning would not be that the child is incapable of understanding salvation, but that the story used did not tell him what salvation is.

One group of children was listening to a man who used magic to try to explain salvation. At the end of his message he asked those who wanted to believe on Jesus to come to the back room with him. Several responded. As these children left that back room, one was heard to say, "Aw shucks, I thought he was going to show us some more tricks." This should cause one to seriously question the use of stories and other lessons that do not mean what they say.

It is true that the Bible contains some symbolism. It is also true that children can understand some symbolism if it is explained to them simply. How much better to spend one's time explaining the symbolism of the Bible in simple, direct terms, rather than to hide the simple truths of the Bible in made-up symbolic stories.

Some Bible stories especially effective in explaining salvation to children are these:

Jesus Talks with Nicodemus, (John, chapter 3)
Jesus Talks with the Woman at the Well of Samaria, (John, chapter 4)
Philip Tells the Ethiopian about Jesus, (Acts, chapter 8)
Paul and Silas Tell a Jailer about Jesus, (Acts 16).

For instance, the story of Nicodemus may be told something like this:

It was night. Nicodemus came to see Jesus. The Bible does not say why Nicodemus came at night. Some people think he came at night because he didn't want anyone to see him, but the Bible doesn't tell us. Perhaps Nicodemus was busy working with his people all day long and could not come until night. Perhaps Jesus was busy teaching and performing miracles all day, and Nicodemus could not talk to Jesus until night. Nicodemus said to Jesus, "We know you are from God.

No one could do the miracles that you do unless he were from God."

Jesus could do wonderful things—things no one else could do. Can you name some of the wonderful things Jesus could do? Yes, he could heal sick people and feed hungry people. Nicodemus knew about some of the miracles that Jesus did, and he knew Jesus was from God.

Then Jesus said something very strange to Nicodemus. Listen to these strange words that Jesus said to him: "Except a man be born again he cannot see the kingdom of God."

Nicodemus could not understand what Jesus meant when he said a person had to be born again in order to see the kingdom of God. Then Jesus said to him, "Don't be surprised that I said, 'You must be born again.' "

These words puzzled Nicodemus. He thought that a person would have to become a tiny baby again. He could not understand how this could be. Nicodemus was a very intelligent man. He knew many things; yet he could not understand what Jesus meant. Today, too, there are many intelligent people who do not understand what Jesus meant when He said, "You must be born again." They are just like Nicodemus. Some of them may be teachers, or doctors, or lawyers. But there are also many intelligent people who do understand what Jesus meant. They might be bankers, or college students, or dentists.

Let us see what Jesus meant when he said, "You must be born again."

Everyone is born as a tiny baby to his mother and father. No one is very big then. When he comes to join his mother and father in a family he is born the first time. Some people are born another time. They are born into God's family. This does not mean that they are tiny babies again. It means that a person believes that Jesus died for his sin. Some persons are four years old when they are born into God's family. Some are six, some nine, some sixteen and some thirty-five or even more.

God wants everyone to be in His family. That is why He sent Jesus to die. The Bible says, "For God so loved the world that he gave his only begotten Son, that whosoever believeth in him should not perish, but have everlasting life." (John 3:16).

How can we be born into God's family? This is an important question because Jesus said that no one can really belong to God unless he is born again. When a person believes on Jesus as his Savior, he is born into God's family.

God's Word, the Bible, says that everyone has sinned. Even children sin. Some say mean things; others disobey parents; others take things that do not belong to them. All these things are wrong. God calls these things sin, and God hates sin. He is perfect, and He cannot stand sin. God loves the world; yet sin must be punished. That is why God sent Jesus to die on the cross for sin. If we want to be born into God's family we must tell Jesus that we are sorry for our sin, and ask Him to forgive our sin. We must believe that His death on the cross counted for us.

This is what Jesus meant when He said those strange words to Nicodemus, "You must be born again."

In comparing the two stories given as examples, one can see that the first one about the ink-stain takes a truth of the Word of God and clothes it in a symbolism that hides, rather than clarifies, the truth. The story of Nicodemus is entirely the Word of God, the parts difficult for the child to grasp being explained by illustrations that the child understands.

It cannot be over-emphasized that it is the Word of God that the Holy Spirit uses, and that if teachers want children to make genuine decisions for Jesus Christ, they must spend their time teaching the Word of God, free from the clutter of man's devices, but full of simple illustrations within the child's experience.

In reference to illustrations, one must remember that stories of children buying their own toys which they had previously lost or of one child taking the punishment of another are illustrations. They are not the message. They might be used within a Bible story to help clarify a point, just as the idea of being born to one's parents was used as an illustration in the account of Nicodemus. But to use them alone as if they were the message is putting the Bible on the shelf. The child must be born into God's family by the use of the Bible, and he must be fed on the Bible if he is ever to grow "unto a perfect man, unto the measure of the stature of the fulness of Christ" (Ephesians 4:13).

One Bible story should be followed by another. At one time the child hears a Bible story, such as about Nicodemus, emphasizing and explaining the necessity of the new birth. At another time he hears the story of the woman at the well, at which time he is taught the meaning of eternal life. Again he hears about Philip and the eunuch, at which time the fact that Jesus was the Christ is stressed. Each story helps the child understand better the message of salvation.

A person cannot say just when the child will grasp the message of salvation clearly enough to actually accept Christ as his Savior. One child may accept Him after one story; another at another time. The teacher must be prepared to help when a child is ready, and willing to wait when a child is not ready. If he is using the Word of God, simply explaining it to the child, he can expect that the Holy Spirit will use that Word to convict. The job is not to figure out gimmicks to cause the child to raise his hand or come to the front; rather the job is to study the Word of God and to study children (most effectively done by being with them) and then to determine ways to help the child understand the Bible. The following will be helpful in determining how to help the child understand:

1. Pray. The teacher needs to pray for insight into the child's needs and abilities. The Lord knows the minds of the very children in any teacher's group. Why can't the teacher talk to Him about them? He needs to pray for guidance in the use of his own time in preparation—that he will use it wisely, that he will not waste it on mere entertainment, that he will be keen to sense which terms and ideas need to be explained and how to explain them. He needs to pray for prepared hearts, not only the children's but his own. Many teachers have experienced the working of the Holy Spirit in one session with children, and somehow felt the lack of such in other sessions, even when preparation and lesson were similar. It is the Lord Himself working in hearts that

makes the difference. The teacher dare not forget this.

2. Listen to the vocabulary of children. What do they talk about? What words do they use? Do they go around talking about burdens, or ropes of sin, the ark of safety, or the sea of life? If those who work with children use expressions not common to the child's everyday speech, those unfamiliar expressions must be explained in terms that the child does use and understand. One needs to be careful not to use too many new expressions in one session, and to repeat in several ways simple meanings for these new thoughts, words, or ideas.

3. Rewrite the Bible story in the child's vocabulary. Follow the story in its context and with its intended meaning. The teacher must be careful not to take one story teaching one truth, and then tell the story tagging on some other truth. If the story emphasizes obedience, obedience should be stressed. If it emphasizes prayer, prayer should be stressed. For instance, in the account of the good Samaritan, (Luke 10:29-37), Jesus is teaching us to have mercy on those who need help. When Jesus used the illustration of the wise man and the foolish man building their houses on the rock and sand, respectively, he was stressing obedience to His commandments, (Matthew 7:24-29). These two accounts, and many others, have either been construed to teach salvation, or a salvation emphasis has been tagged on the end. If the teacher will rewrite the account in a child's language, simply following the words of Scripture, and looking for the main teaching of the passage, he will be less likely to misuse the Word of God. Some are so eager to press salvation that they forget everything else the Bible teaches. Of course it is important to stress the need for salvation, but it is equally im-

portant to base that teaching on a passage of Scripture which teaches salvation.

It will be well for the teacher to check any prepared lessons with the Scripture upon which the lesson is based to see that the lesson actually teaches the central truth of the passage used. When the Word of God is given forth as the Word of God, one can expect that it will be received as the Word of God. (See I Thessalonians 2, especially verses 3-5, 13, for an instance in which this happened.) If a child is brought up on teaching in which he gets the central truth of any passage under consideration, he will grow into a well-developed Christian with a good understanding of the whole of the Bible. Indeed he will be a better Christian worker, even pastor, if that should be his work; for if he is fed on central truths, he will feed others that way. It is shallow, and perhaps even dangerous, teaching that thinks of an idea and then grasps for a verse or passage on which to hang it. The one who thinks of himself as teaching the Bible should start with the Bible, stay with the Bible, end with the Bible, and explain the Bible. This does not mean that he cannot use illustrations. Illustrations are good, in fact often necessary, but they must be in line with the central truth of the passage if that truth is to be grasped by the pupils. All of these things must be kept in mind and followed if the story rewritten in the child's language is to "line up" with the teaching of the chosen passage.

4. Do not be limited to plot stories. It is not necessary to plan every session with children around a story that has a hero, a conflict, an introduction, climax, and closing, such as a plot story has. If one is limited to plot stories, one of two things will happen:

(a) Some parts of Scripture will be omitted even though a child could understand them.

(b) These accounts will be forced into plot stories.

Psalm 115 is not difficult for children to understand. It is not a plot story; it is not actually a story at all. Yet children can read some parts for themselves, especially verses 4-8.

John 1:1-14 and John 10:1-21 are not plot stories; yet they should neither be omitted nor made into such stories. Passages such as these can be read thought by thought and talked over with the children. The children can be asked questions; and they can ask questions in learning what these portions say and mean. True, there are several parts of each of these passages that will need to be explained clearly in the child's vocabulary and experiences in order for him to understand them. This is one reason it is good to talk over the portions with the children; then the teacher can sense the child's understanding or misunderstanding of the Bible.

IV. GIVING INVITATIONS

WHEN ONE faithfully teaches the word of God to children, explaining each truth clearly, he need not force or push for decisions. However, he should be ready always for any child with whom the Holy Spirit may be working.

Some Scripture passages lend themselves more easily to invitations to accept Christ than others. When such invitations are given, they should be based on Scripture emphasizing salvation. Other principles in giving invitations to accept Christ as Savior include these:

1. Make the invitation clear, so that the child knows what he is responding to. A child's mind easily wanders, and he may respond just because other children do, especially if he does not clearly understand the issue.

In one instance, three children responded when asked if they wanted to become Christians. The teacher in talking with them afterwards asked, "Can any of you tell me why you came into this room with me just now? One of the children said, "To hear more stories." Another answered, "To sing songs about Jesus."

2. Be ready any time. The child should understand that he can come with his questions about salvation, or other things, at any time. This means that the teacher cannot be in a hurry to leave, for if he is, he will assign certain times at which the child may be saved. No one can do this. The child is quick to sense whether or not his teacher is available. The child may ask about salvation even when an invitation as such has not been given. One time a teacher was right in the middle of an Old Testament character study with his

class when one of the boys said, "Mr. W________, when the other kids are having handwork, can I accept the Lord?" Thus it was. After the Bible study and discussion was over, and the others were working on handcrafts, Bobby sat in one corner with Mr. W________ and accepted Jesus Christ as his Savior.

3. Invite the children to talk to you individually. Each child has different needs and different questions. Also if the children are asked to come individually, they are more likely to come because they really sense a need to accept Christ than if they are just asked to stand or to raise their hands.

4. Avoid making the invitation so easy that the acceptance of it is not real. Ask those who want to accept Christ as Savior to stay while others go to recess. If the Holy Spirit is dealing with them, they will stay. One time when this was done, one child stayed. Then after recess another child came to the teacher, and said, "You haven't talked to me yet." The teacher helped the children get started on their memory verse drill, turned that session over to her co-worker, and went to another place with the child, where that child, too, accepted Jesus as Savior. Sometimes it seems that people are not willing to trust the Holy Spirit to work. They seem to think that unless they push and push they are not doing their job. Yet it has been the experience of the author that a child will come seeking help after a recess or after some other activity. One child even came a whole day after a lesson on how one becomes a Christian.

5. Be sensitive to the Holy Spirit's guidance. This guidance is necessary in both teacher and pupil. The teacher needs to be in an attitude of prayer as the invitation is given.

Besides this, he should be in the attitude of prayer during his preparation and during the entire lesson, so that the Holy Spirit can actually use every part of the lesson, not just the last few lines.

V. WHAT TO DO WHEN A CHILD WANTS TO ACCEPT JESUS CHRIST

AFTER A LESSON is taught and a child indicates that he wants to become a Christian, then what? These suggestions will help as to what should be done:

1. Talk with the child alone, if at all possible. If he is from a Christian home, his background and understanding will be different from that of a child with no Christian environment in his home. Even children from Christian families, indeed, two children from the same family, have different questions. Talking with a child alone gives the teacher opportunity to ask questions, to let the child ask questions, and to learn what ideas might need to be cleared up in the child's thinking later on.

2. Ask him questions. Such questions as these might be used: Have you ever talked with someone about accepting Jesus as your Savior before? What is sin? Why did Jesus die? What do you need to do to become a Christian? What does this verse say? What does it mean? These questions will, of course, not always be used in this order. Some of them may not be used at all. The use of questions helps child and teacher talk together. It keeps the child's attention on what is being said. It helps him think through what he is doing. It helps the teacher sense whether the child is grasping the truth or not.

3. Take time. Do not be in a hurry. It takes time to talk with the child, to listen to what he has to say, to ask him questions, to answer his questions. If a teacher wants to, he can get a child to repeat three lines of a prayer, one at a time, after him, and then tell the child he is a Christian;

and the child will, for a time, think that was his Christian experience. However, the object is not to get the child to go through certain motions, but to help him understand the significance of Christ's death for him, and to help him to actually accept Christ as Savior.

4. Use the Bible. If the child has a Bible, it is best to use his. If he can read, he should be allowed to read the verses himself; if not, the teacher can read them to him. One verse should be read and talked about at a time. If the Bible the child has is his own, rather than the expensive family Bible, the verses can be marked or listed in the front. Otherwise, colored strips of paper can be put in the proper places. The papers may be used in the child's own Bible too, if he has difficulty finding the verses.

5. Use only a few verses. If too many verses are used, the child is confused. See chapter I for some verses that might be used. Others, besides those, might be John 14:6, Acts 16.31, Romans 10:9-10. The teacher should be familiar with several in order to use the ones that fit best for each pupil.

6. Ask the child to pray. Do not be surprised if he says "I don't know what to say." Talk it over with him, perhaps using questions again, such as these: Do you think you should tell Jesus that you are sorry for your sin? Should you ask Him to forgive you? Do you want to tell Him that you want His death on the cross to count for you? After a few questions, the child may be ready to pray. If not, he may pray after the teacher, line by line. If he and his teacher have talked it over, he understands better what he is saying, even if he says it line by line after the teacher, than he would if he just repeated parrot-fashion without talking it over. In

many cases, after the little talk with the teacher, the child will feel more at ease, and will pray on his own.

7. Talk further with him. Ask him more questions: What did you just do? Did Jesus forgive your sins? How do you know? If someone asks you if you are a Christian, what will you say? What if he says, "How do you know?" Direct the child to use his Bible as he answers these questions. He can take his Bible with him; he cannot take his teacher; and he needs the source for his answers with him.

8. Remember him. When a child accepts Christ as Savior, the teacher's job is not done. A big job is just begun. The child needs to be taught. He should be visited. He needs to learn to pray, to read his Bible, and to live a life pleasing to God. Many children are sent away, after accepting Christ, with these words, "Now you are a Christian. You must pray and read your Bible every day." That is all the follow-up they get from the one who led them to Christ. The Apostle Paul did not even treat grown-ups so lightly. He wrote to them; he prayed for them; he taught them; he sent others to visit them; he went to visit them himself. (See Philippians 1:4; 2:12-23, for example.)

The child needs someone to help him memorize a Scripture verse, to pray with him, to ask him occasionally, "What did you read in the Bible today?" or "What did you do today to show that you love Jesus?" He needs someone to show him what to read in the Bible. Some of his favorite Bible stories might be easiest at first. His previous acquaintance with them will help him read, and if he is using the King James Version, will help him become acquainted with the language of that version. Some persons actually sound quite spiritual when they say, "The child is a Christian now. He can be trusted to God, for now he has the discernment of

the Holy Spirit." True, the Christian does have the discernment of the Holy Spirit, but it is the Word of God that the
Holy Spirit uses to cause one to discern. If a person does
not know what the Bible says, it is difficult to live according to its teachings.

The teacher should also pray for the child who has accepted Christ. He needs someone to pray about the prob-
lems he has; perhaps others in his family are not Christians;
he needs someone to pray for them.

The follow-up work with a child is not to be taken lightly. If the new Christian is to be able to follow Colos-
sians 2:6, "As ye have therefore received Christ Jesus
the Lord, so walk in him," the Christian worker will
have to take the responsibility implied in 2:7. He
will have to do some teaching in order that the other
can be rooted and built up in Christ. Note the responsibility suggested in that and in the following verse. "Rooted
and built up in him, and stablished in the faith, *as ye have
been taught,* abounding therein with thanksgiving. Beware
lest any man spoil you through philosophy and vain deceit,
after the tradition of men, after the rudiments of the world,
and not after Christ" (Col. 2:7-8). How will the new Christian be rooted and built up in Christ if he is not taught? How
will he abound in thanksgiving if he is not taught? How will
he recognize the philosophy and deceit of the world if he
is not taught? How will he know whether his acts, words,
and thoughts are after Christ if he is not taught? Who is
going to do the teaching?

There are many portions in the New Testament that
show that God's way, the way Paul followed, in reaching
others for Christ was not the "win 'em and leave 'em" type of
evangelism. (If such were Paul's philosophy, we would not

have the epistles of the New Testament!) Dare we take an attitude different from Paul's toward those who accept Christ under our ministry?

God has called us as co-workers with Him. Let us do our best, considering those to whom He has sent us, their interests, abilities, and needs; the tool He has given, His own Word; and the source of power, the Holy Spirit. Let us remember all of these as we go forth to help children understand the Word of God, and through that understanding, to come to know Christ as Savior, to grow up in Him, and then to serve Him.

FOR FURTHER READING

God Loves Me. Upper Darby, Pennsylvania: Bible Club Movement Publications, 1977.

> A tract-like booklet based on John 3:16. Explains each part of the verse clearly. Illustrated with pictures to talk about with the child as one proceeds.

God Wants You to Be a Member of His Family and Grow As His Child. Glendale, California: Gospel Light Publications.

> A small illustrated booklet that children can read for themselves. Good to use in talking to individual children about their relationship with Jesus Christ.

LeBar, Mary B. *Living in God's Family.* Wheaton, Illinois: Scripture Press, 1957.

> This book is written for children, especially for those who have just accepted Christ as Savior. It explains salvation simply in the child's language. Teachers should encourage children to read it. Teachers themselves will find it helpful in knowing how to explain salvation in the way a child understands it.

Marxhausen, Joanne. *If I Should Live; If I Should Die.* St. Louis, Missouri: Concordia Publishing House, 1975.

> Helps the child understand why Jesus had to die, His perfect life, His living again, and what heaven is like. Shows that Jesus' living in one results in living forever in heaven, but will need some explanation as to how Jesus comes to live inside a person. Only a few words on a page. A second grade child can read most words. Illustrated.

McDaniel, Elsiebeth. *How to Become God's Child and Live in His Family.* Wheaton, Illinois: Scripture Press Publication, 1970.

> An illustrated book with about 12 by 18 inch pages for teachers and parents to use with children. Uses simple non-symbolic language in telling a child how to become God's child. A small copy of the book is available to give to

children after a group presentation of the message. It contains the entire story of the larger book and is good for use with individual children.

Soderholm, Marjorie. *Understanding the Pupil.* Grand Rapids, Michigan: Baker Book House, 1955, 1956.

This is a series of three books, one on the Pre-School Child; one on the Primary and Junior Child; and one on the Adolescent. Helps the adult understand the child or young person in five areas: physical, mental, social, emotional, and spiritual. Gives many actual illustrations of things children and young people say and do.

Soderholm, Marjorie. *Salvation, Then What?* Minneapolis, Minnesota: Free Church Publications, 1968.

A follow-up manual on *Explaining Salvation to Children.* Makes specific suggestions to those working with children, helping them in knowing how to encourage a child to grow in his Christian life. Special sections for the teacher, the pastor, and the camp counselor. Includes a bibliography of materials for those working with children, books for the child himself to use, and a list of tracts to use with children who have accepted Christ.